The Far Side® GALLERY 3

The Far Side® G·A·L·L·E·R·Y 3

by Gary Larson

Andrews McMeel
Publishing, LLC
Kansas City

For information, write Andrews McMeel Publishing, LLC, an Andrews McMeel Universal company, 1130 Walnut Street, Kansas City, Missouri 64106

www.andrewsmcmeel.com

ISBN-13: 978-0-7407-8996-0
ISBN-10: 0-7407-8996-1

For Jimmy D'Aquisto —
artist, philosopher, and friend

FOREWORD

I'm a paleontologist and taxonomist; I study land snails. Hey, I know why they asked my buddy Steve King to write the foreword to the last volume; he's supposed to know something about humor in the macabre style. But I feel like Marvelous Marv Throneberry, most inept of the hapless original Mets, who made some beer commercials a few years back and ended each appearance by saying: "I don't know why they asked me to make this ad." I mean, I don't know from funny; I study snails.

But I do observe the social life of laboratories and scientific offices, and I know something remarkable (and worthy of sharing) about Gary Larson, something essentially unknown outside my parish. Scientists are an idiosyncratic lot; we almost make a fetish of our individuality. When we all move cowlike in a certain direction not dictated by inexorable facts of nature — well, that is a sociological incident worth recording. Something amazing has happened to the doors and bulletin boards of academic corridors in the natural sciences. These blank spaces are traditionally festooned with bits of humor chosen to make statements about serious issues in science or laboratory life. In keeping with our cussed independence, these items have been as varied as their selectors. But a Gary Larson virus is spreading throughout the country. No kidding and no exaggeration; I think that about eighty percent of my colleagues' doors now sport a Larson cartoon. No fewer than twenty correspondents have sent me the smoking sauropods with the caption, "The real reason dinosaurs became extinct" —all thinking that they were doing something original. This situation creates a damnable problem for me. I can think of a dozen or two items in this book that I'd love to put on my door. But I can't for fear of conformity.

I also think I know why Gary Larson is *numero uno* by a mile among my colleagues — and that gives me something to write about. Being funny is surely a criterion, but simple chuckles do not explain why we have spontaneously chosen Gary Larson as national humorist of natural history. He has won by informal acclamation because he understands science so well. And I don't mean factual knowledge (this is available for the asking from textbooks and courses); I refer to the subtle nuances and insights — hundreds of them, sometimes several per cartoon — showing that Gary Larson knows the intimate details of our daily lives and practices.

Since I am a taxonomist by profession, and since vague generalizations are so useless, let me illustrate my point with examples from this volume arranged as a classification. Animals go in categories because the history of life is a branching tree, but ideas are all over the place in anastomosing networks — and they therefore defy classification. I choose five categories for my purposes; others would use fewer or more, drawn on differing bases.

Gary Larson is a natural historian. The foibles of human relationships with the natural world, and the bad habits of culture and society thus reflected, provide his central theme. In my first two categories, he places animals into human situations — using the differences to show how less than logical or universal our unquestioned practices can be.

In the first category of human social behaviors exposed by changing the species involved, three dour-faced committee members recline on the dais while parent fish speak at a microphone from the audience. The title: "The committee to decide whether spawning should be taught in school" (a lovely second pun given the choice of animal subject). In another, dogs sit in a crowded movie theater, all looking one way, then all looking the other way. The caption reads "At the popular dog film, *Man Throwing Sticks*." My favorite has (and needs) no title. A large baited mousetrap ominously occupies the foreground. A group of mice are bowing, chanting, and gesticulating in some dark pagan ritual. On a platform, heading for sacrifice, sits a female mouse festooned with beads and sporting a magnificent hairdo. A lovely commentary on the virgin-in-volcano-to-appease-the-firegod ritual scene of those old bwana hero films once so beloved in Hollywood.

A second category recognizes that language is not a neutral medium of optimal communication, but also a reservoir of illogic, cultural chauvinism, and literally senseless cliché. A child sits by a television with his sibling, a half creature cleaved right down the middle — all to illustrate the "average size" American family, and to make a telling point about the differences between mean values and actual circumstances. A group of soldiers attempt to piece the jigsaw puzzle of an egg-man together, while a group of horses wait their turn. "All the king's horses" in connection with Humpty Dumpty never did make any sense. A distraught elk reads a letter from his now ex-

girlfriend, lamenting the "John deer" message that it contains.

Three other categories comment directly upon science, rather than simply using the objects of natural history to expose human foibles. One group treats the "myths" of science—either falsehoods perpetrated by common wisdom, or basic truths so often repeated that they become clichés divorced from their true significance, and therefore objects of Larson's instructive and revealing wit. A dog breaks a mirror and then punctures the nonsense about one dog year equaling seven human years of lifespan by lamenting that he will have forty-nine years of bad luck. A man in a rubber boat labeled "Norm's Spawning Service" takes a group of tired salmon upstream—so much for our cultural symbol of self-sacrificing persistence in pursuit of the greatest reward of all. Two illicit penguin lovers part from each other amidst a forest of lookalikes, and one says: "I have to go, Charles... Frank is getting more and more suspicious." No, they don't all look the same, and neither do blacks or orientals (or whites like me to others, for that matter).

A second set treats concepts in such a subtle way that Gary clearly understands both the ideas and their problems every bit as well as we do. Consider just a few from his "caveman" series, each really a commentary on our cardinal cultural shibboleth of "progress." Cave bears disperse a motley rabble of primitive hunters, but not without noting: "Criminy! It seems like every summer there's more and more of these things around." A pair of our ancestral heroes down a mammoth with one arrow to the underside. One says to the other: "Maybe we should write that spot down." Serious adaptationist theories about the origin of language suggest exactly this, though for speech rather than for writing. In my favorite, three bewildered cavemen sit on a ledge playing the primitive version of the kiddie hand-game paper-rock-scissors. But since paper and scissors have not yet been invented, they only know the symbol for rock, and every match ends in a tie—to their confusion and frustration.

A last category, my favorite, treats the arcana of science—the little bits known only to professionals who lead the life, and therefore winning for Larson an entry into the priesthood of our inner sanctum. Perhaps these are not so universally accessible, but Larson carefully structures these pieces on two levels, so that you see the humor even if you don't know the full context, but really guffaw if you do. Two groups of astronomers battle before a telescope under the caption: "All day long, a tough gang of astrophysicists would monopolize the telescope and intimidate the other researchers." Funny enough by itself (especially given the limited use of the machine during daylight hours), but if you know that telescopes are in desperately short supply, and that scientists (particularly Ph.D. students low on the totem pole) often wait months for a few hours of evening viewing (tough darts, and back to "go," if it's cloudy), then the point really sinks in.

In another wonderfully subtle comment, a horse teacher gives instruction in arithmetic to three youngsters: "So if I have four apples and I give two away, how many do I have left?" In the bottom section, the students give their answers by tapping their hooves the right (but in each case here, the wrong) number of times on the desk. Funny by itself? Yes. But the cartoon is a commentary on the famous case of "Clever Hans," a horse who could do arithmetic according to some mystics, psychics, and other life forms at the scientific fringe. Hans worked by pawing the ground with his hoof until he reached the right answer. Hans may even have fooled his trainer into thinking he understood arithmetic, but it turned out that the trainer was unconsciously cueing Hans to stop by changing his facial gestures after the right number of paw strokes. Hans showed enormously subtle understanding in his reading of facial gestures, but he couldn't do arithmetic. Animals have intelligences different from ours; they are not just primitive models of our achievements.

Everyone has a favorite based on his own career — and I expect that the items on doors of my colleagues are personal statements. I think we all feel that Gary made one just for us. In mine, a group of Protozoa are watching a slide show, and one says: "No, wait! That's not Uncle Floyd! Who is that? Criminy, I think it's just an air bubble!" Why did this put me supine in the aisles? Well, when I took embryology in college, we had to make serial sections through a chick embryo. I made a technically perfect set of sections; I was so proud. But when I put my product under the microscope, I discovered that I had made a perfect serial section through an air bubble, and caught the embryo at some useless angle. I abandoned laboratory work and became a paleontologist.

One final comment that says it all. It is the caption of another Protozoan cartoon, but take it more generally as the real reason, not only for Gary Larson's success, but for the deep respect that he has won from us: Two amoebae are watching television, and one says to the other: "Stimulus, response! Stimulus, response! Don't you ever *think*?" Most of us live like the amoebae, but Larson won't let us. There is no more important intellectual lesson, however it be taught.

— STEPHEN JAY GOULD
  Museum of Comparative Zoology
  Harvard University

"Ooo! *This* is always amusing.... Here comes Bessie inside her plastic cow ball."

"Hey, bucko…I'm *through* begging."

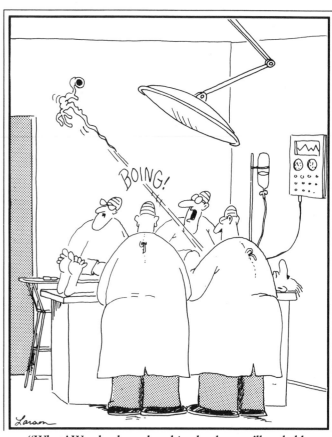

"Whoa! Watch where that thing lands — we'll probably need it."

Roberta takes on a dust rhino.

"She's lookin' good, Vern!"

Dirk brings his family tree to class.

Bobbing for poodles

"Hold it right there, Doreen!...Leave if you must — but the dog *stays*!"

"Holy moley, Loretta! Not only is it still there, look what it did to the end of my stick!"

Alien family dinners

Through some unfortunate celestial error, Ernie is sent to Hog Heaven.

18

Never put your tongue on a glacier.

June 24, 1876: Custer's last group photo

Chicken nudist colonies

"So! Planning on roaming the neighborhood with some of your buddies today?"

"Hey, Johnny! This lady wants to know the difference in all these fertilizers!"

"It's back, Arnie! Get the book!...We're gonna settle whether it's an alligator or a crocodile once and for all!"

"Wait a minute, Vince! Last summer—remember? Some little kid caught you, handled you, and tossed you back in the swamp...*That's* where you got 'em."

"Well, I'll be...Honey, it's the Worthingtons—our favorite couple of slimebags."

"Yo! Farmer Dave! Let's go, let's go, let's go!... You gettin' up with us chickens or not?"

"Buffalo breath? *Buffalo* breath?... Shall we discuss your incessant little *grunting* noises?"

"For heaven's sake, Henry, tell the kids a *pleasant* story for once — they don't always have to hear the one about your head."

"Oh, wonderful! Look at this, Etta — another mouth to feed."

"Well, there goes *my* appetite."

Cat showers

Rusty makes his move.

Secret tools of the common crow

Primitive mobsters

Final page of the Medical Boards

"Well, if I'm lucky, I should be able to get off this thing in about six more weeks."

"Well, shoot! *There's* my herd!... Thank you anyway, ma'am."

In that one split second, when the choir's last note had ended, but before the audience could respond, Vinnie Conswego belches the phrase, "That's all, folks."

"My God! Willard's home early! Don't move — his vision's not very good, but his sense of smell and hearing are quite acute."

Dizzy Gillespie's seventh birthday party

"For crying out loud, I was *hibernating*!.... Don't you guys ever take a pulse?"

"Goldberg, you idiot! Don't play tricks on those things — they can't distinguish between 'laughing with' and 'laughing at'!"

"And when the big moment comes, here's the nursery Robert and I have fixed up."

"Johnson, back off! It's an *Armandia lidderdalii*, all right — but it's rabid!"

"Well, one guess which table wants another round of banana daiquiris."

"Raised the ol' girl from a cub, I did…'Course, we had to get a few things straight between us. She don't try to follow me into town anymore, and I don't try and take her food bowl away 'til she's done."

The Bluebird of Happiness long absent from his life, Ned is visited by the Chicken of Depression.

"'You have a small capacity for reason, some basic tool-making skills, and the use of a few simple words.'... Yep. That's you."

The monster snorkel: Allows your child to breathe comfortably without exposing vulnerable parts to an attack.

Early wheeler-dealers

Horror films of the wild

"Barbara! I'm goin' for help — tread soup!"

"Well, let's see — so far I've got rhythm, I've got music...actually, who could ask for anything more?"

Second to last of the Mohicans

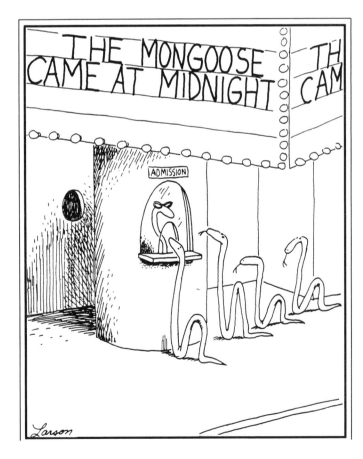

"Oh my God! It's from Connie! She's written me a 'John deer' letter!"

"Of course, long before you mature, most of you will be eaten."

"You wanna have some fun, Fred? Watch...Growling and bristling, I'm gonna stand in front of the closet door and just stare."

"Oh, please, Mom!...I've already handled him and now the mother won't take him back."

"One bee!…One lousy little bee gets inside and you just lose it!"

"Whoa! Smells like a French primate house in here."

"You know, it was supposed to be just a story about a little kid and a wolf…but off and on, I've been dressing up as a grandmother ever since."

"Stimulus, response! Stimulus, response! Don't you ever *think*?"

Midway through the exam, Allen pulls out a bigger brain.

The Hendersons of the jungle

"Mr. Mathews! Mr. Mathews! I just came back from the restroom and Hodges here took my seat!...It's my turn for the window seat, Mr. Mathews!"

Suddenly, through forces not yet fully understood, Darren Belsky's apartment became the center of a new black hole.

"Boy, he even looks like a drowned rat."

"Ohhhhhh…Look at that, Schuster…Dogs are so cute when they try to comprehend quantum mechanics."

"Oh, Ginger—you look absolutely stunning…and whatever you rolled in sure does stink."

"Think about it, Murray.…If we could get this baby runnin,' we could run over hikers, pick up females, chase down mule deer—man, we'd be the grizzlies from hell."

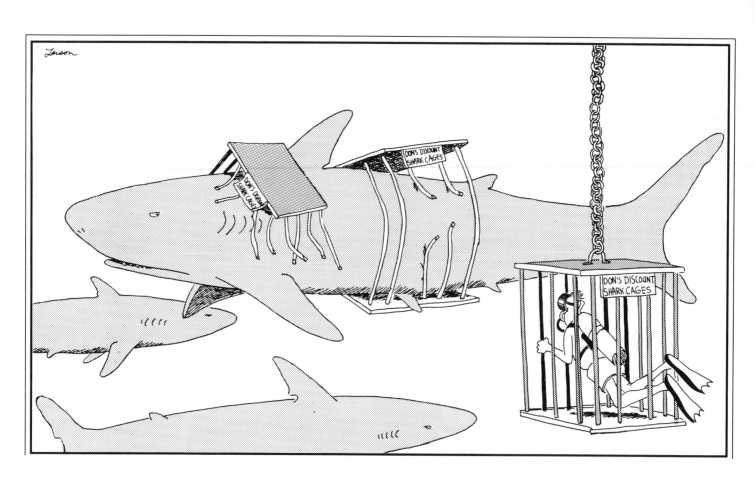

Moby's parents

"There it is again...a feeling that in a past life I was someone named Shirley MacLaine."

Fly whimsy

"My boy made the frame."

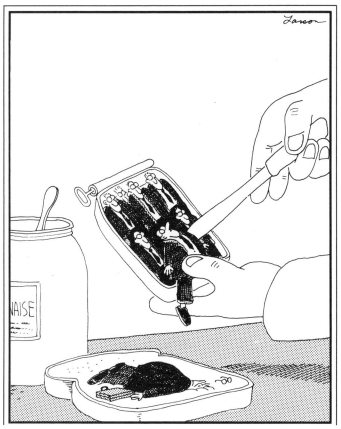

Business lunch

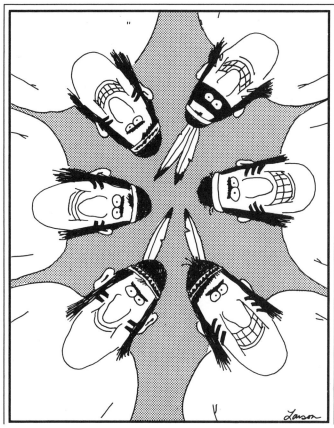

Custer's last view

Places never to set your electric eel

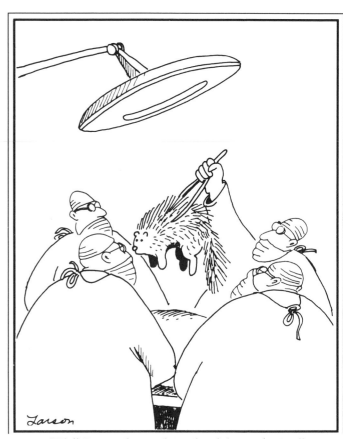

"Well, I guess that explains the abdominal pains."

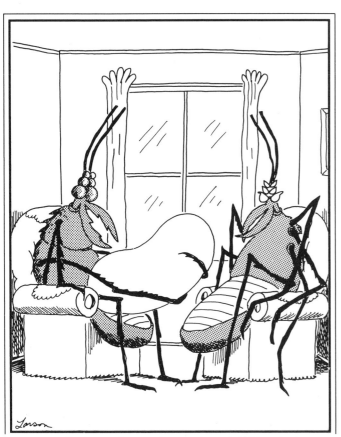

"Well, Roger's hoping for a male and I'd like a little female....But, really, we'll both be content if it just has six eyes and eight legs."

"I heard that, Simmons! I'm a wimp, am I?...Well, to heck with you — to heck with *all* of you!"

50,000 B.C.: Gak Eisenberg invents the first and last silent mammoth whistle.

To win the tribe's respect, Jed first had to defeat their best thumb-wrestler.

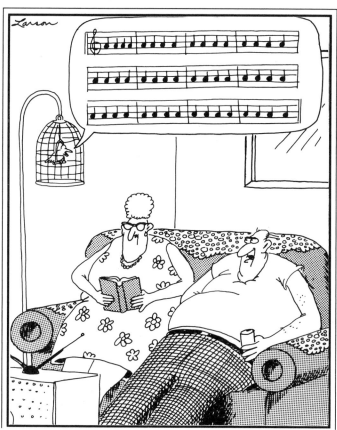

"Hit the bird, Ruth — he's stuck."

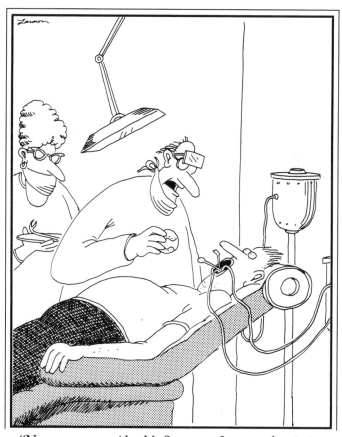

"Now open even wider, Mr. Stevens.... Just out of curiosity, we're going to see if we can also cram in this tennis ball."

Rocking the anthropological world, a second "Lucy" is discovered in southern Uganda.

"And that's the hand that fed me."

Although troubled as a child, Zorro, as is well known, ultimately found his niche in history.

Night of the Potato Bugs

"In the wild, of course, they'd be natural enemies — but they do just fine together if you get 'em as pups."

"OK, guys, let's move in on those three heifers in the corner…. Bob, you take the 'Triple R,' Dale, you take the 'Circle L,' and I'll take the 'Lazy Q!'"

"OK, folks!…It's a wrap!"

"Oh, my! Aren't *these* fancy drinks!

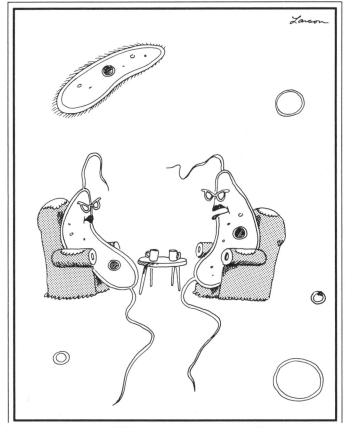

"He told you *that*? Well, he's pulling your flagellum, Nancy."

The rural professional and his cowphone

Non-singing canaries have to take wood shop.

Embarrassing moments at gene parties

The townsfolk all stopped and stared; they didn't know the tall stranger who rode calmly through their midst, but they did know the reign of terror had ended.

"Uh-oh, Danny. Sounds like the monster in the basement has heard you crying again....Let's be reaaaal quiet and hope he goes away."

How fishermen blow their own minds

"Sidney, just take one…Don't handle every fly."

"So, then, when Old MacDonald turned his back, I took that ax, and with a whack whack here and a whack whack there, I finished him off."

Neither rain nor snow nor sleet nor hail, they said, could stop the mail.…But they didn't figure on Rexbo.

"It's this new boyfriend, dear....I'm just afraid one day your father's going to up and blow him away."

Where "minute" steaks come from

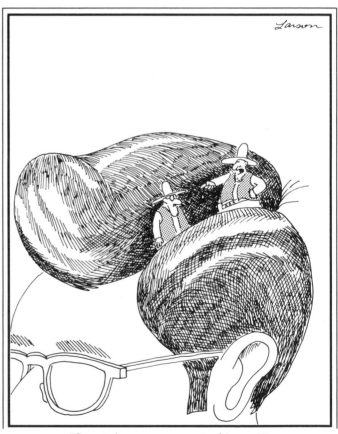

"Say, ain't you a stranger in this part?"

"Drive, George, drive! This one's got a coat hanger!"

"You call this a niche?"

Snake weight-rooms

"Bob and Ruth! Come on in.... Have you met Russell and Bill, our 1.5 children?"

Chicken cults

"Beats me how they did it...I got the whole thing at a garage sale for five bucks — and that included the stand."

"OK, sir, would you like inferno or non-inferno?...Ha! Just kidding. It's all inferno, of course — I just get a kick out of saying that."

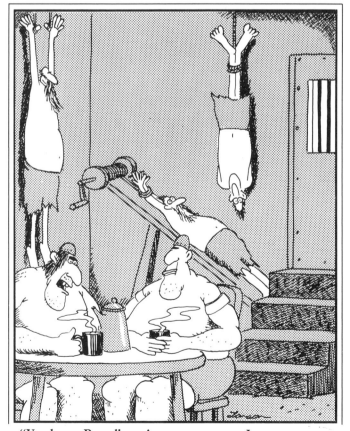

"Ernie! Look what you're doing — take those shoes off!"

Washington crossing the street

"You know, Russell, you're a great torturer. I mean, you can make a man scream for mercy in nothing flat... but boy, you sure can't make a good cup of coffee."

And then, just as he predicted, Thag became the channeler for a two million-year-old gibbon named Gus.

Suddenly, Dr. Frankenstein realized he had left his brain in San Francisco.

"Oh, and here's Luanne now. . . . Bobby just got sheared today, Luanne."

Inside the sun

"OK, let's take a look at you."

"And so you just threw everything together? ... Mathews, a posse is something you have to *organize*."

"This is it, Jenkins. ... Indisputable proof that the Ice Age caught these people completely off guard."

The Snakes of War

Anthro horror films

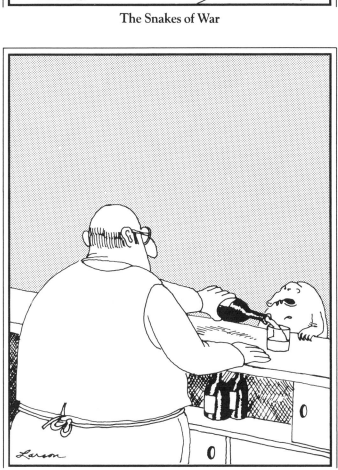

"Sho I sez to her, 'Hey, look! I'm tired of living in this hole, digging dirt, and eating worms!'"

Helen paused. With an audible "wumph," Muffy's familiar yipping had ended, and only the sounds of Ed's football game now emanated from the living room.

Dog endorsements

"And now that's the last of that."

The secret python burial grounds

Animal horoscopes

"Gee, that's a wonderful sensation....Early in the morning, you just woke up, you're tired, movin' kinda slow, and then that oooooold smell hits your nose — blood in the water."

"Ha! Figured you might try escapin', Bert — so I just took the liberty of removin' your horse's brain."

Amoeba conventions

"Uh-oh, Norm. Across the street — whale-watchers."

"I hear 'em!... Gee, there must be a *hundred* of the little guys squirmin' around in there!"

"Shoot! Drain's clogged.... Man, I hate to think what might be down there."

"Oh my God!...Murray's attacking the bathroom mirror!"

"Henry! Hurry or you're gonna miss it — ghost riders in the kitchen!"

When jellyfish travel at unsafe speeds

"Margaret! He's doing it! He's doing it!"

"No, he's not busy...in fact, that whole thing is just a myth."

"And here we are last summer going south....Wait a minute, Irene! We went *north* last summer! The stupid slide's in backward!"

Going out for the evening, Tarzan and Jane forget to tie up the dog.

Shark Food-fights

Cow joyrides

Simultaneously all three went for the ball, and the coconut-like sound of their heads colliding secretly delighted the bird.

"Mom said no sitting on the edge, Wayne."

"Randy! Just sit down, eat your cereal, and look for that thing later!"

"Now!"

Another case of too many scientists and not enough hunchbacks

The Pillsbury Doughboy meets Frank's Asphalt and Concrete Paving Service.

"Again? You just had a glass of water 12 days ago."

"Come on, baby... One grunt for Daddy... one grunt for Daddy."

In the Old West, vegetarians were often shot with little provocation.

"And here we are last summer off the coast of... Helen, is this Hawaii or Florida?"

"Hey c'mon! Don't put your mouth on it!"

"Won't talk, huh?...Frankie! Hand me that scaler."

"Mr. Osborne, may I be excused? My brain is full."

Early chemists describe the first dirt molecule.

Snake horror stories

"Well, the sloth nailed him...y'know, ol' Hank never was exactly a 'quick draw.'"

"Hey, Norton!...Ain't that your dog attackin' the president?"

The operation was a success: Later, the duck, with his new human brain, went on to become the leader of a great flock. Irwin, however, was ostracized by his friends and family and eventually just wandered south.

When piranha dine out

A young Genghis Khan and his Mongol hordette

Brain aerobics

Parents of a lazy river

"C'mon, c'mon!...Either it's here or it isn't!"

"For crying out loud, Warren...can't you just beat your chest like everyone else?"

Inadvertently, Roy dooms the entire earth to annihilation when, in an attempt to be friendly, he seizes their leader by the head and shakes vigorously.

"Blow, Howie, blow!...Yeah, yeah, yeah! You're cookin' now, Howie!...All right!...Charlie Parker, move over!...Yeah!"

"It's 'Them,' gentlemen."

At the Strategic Pie Limitation Talks

"How many times did I say it, Harold? How many times? 'Make sure that bomb shelter's got a can opener — ain't much good without a can opener,' I said."

"Well, sorry about this, Mrs. Murdoch, but old Roy and I got to arguin' politics, and dang if he didn't say some things that got my adrenalin flowin'."

In God's den

Man, Bernie, you're a mess!... You ain't itchin' anywhere, are you? Man, I had a cast on my leg years ago and <u>boy</u> did it itch!...Drove me crazy! Y'know what I'm sayin'?... 'Cause you can't scratch it, y'know... Don't think about itching anywhere, Bernie, 'cause it'll drive you <u>nuts</u>!

"Well, wouldn't you know it — we've come all this way to our favorite beach and someone's strung chicken wire around it."

Cattle humor

"Hey, Bob wants in — does anyone know how to work this thing?"

Buddy's dreams

Ornithology 101 field trips

Killer bees are generally described as starting out as larvae delinquents.

"Say, Will — why don't you pull that thing out and play us a tune?"

At the Vincent van Gogh School of Art

The primitive game of "Kiss-the-mammoth-and-run"

"Sorry to bother you, sir, but there's another salesman out here — you want me to tell him to go to heaven?"

"More worms?…Saaaaaaaaay — why are you being so nice to me all of a sudden?"

Before paper and scissors

Mr. Ed spills his guts.

"Vince! Just trample him!…He's drawing you into his kind of fight!"

"Gad, that's eerie…no matter where you stand the nose seems to follow."

Crow kids

"Looks like some drifter comin' into town."

"Hey! What's this, Higgins? Physics equations?...Do you enjoy your job here as a cartoonist, Higgins?"

Their reunion was both brief and awkward — each still bearing the wounds from that ugly "Jane incident."

"You know what I'm sayin'? Me, for example. I couldn't work in some stuffy little office…. The outdoors just calls to me."

"Grog…They play our song."

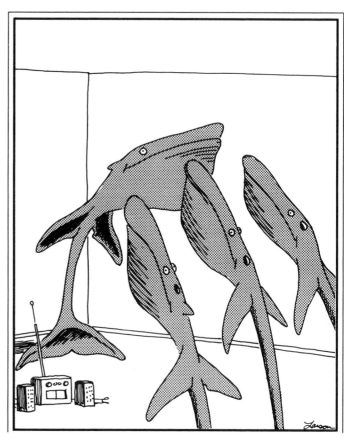

Whale fitness classes

The embarrassment of riding off into a fake sunset

Some of the non-vital organs

Volume five in a series

Mutants on the *Bounty*

How cow documentaries are made

Professor Gallagher and his controversial technique of simultaneously confronting the fear of heights, snakes, and the dark.

"So, you're a *real* gorilla, are you? Well, guess you wouldn't mind munchin' down a few beetle grubs, would you?...In fact, we wanna see you chug 'em!"

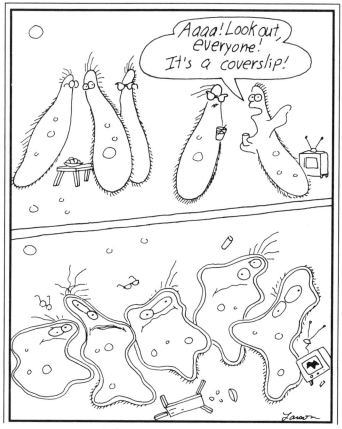

Life on a microscope slide

Products that prey on shark wimps

"It's Bob, all right...but look at those vacuous eyes, that stupid grin on his face — he's been domesticated, I tell you."

"Listen. I've *tried* to communicate with him, but he's like a broken record: 'None of your bee's wax, none of your bee's wax.'"

In the early days, living in their squalid apartment, all three shared dreams of success. In the end, however, Bob the Spoon and Ernie the Fork wound up in an old silverware drawer, and only Mac went on to fame and fortune.

The Headless Horsefamily

94

"Forget these guys."

In the Fly House of Horrors

"And *you*, Johnson! You stick with your man and keep that hand in his *face*!"

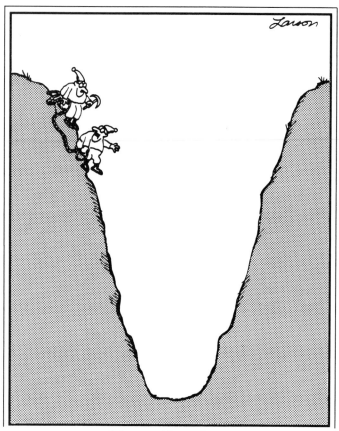

"Because it's not there."

Clumsy ghosts

"Tough break, Rusty.... Seven years bad luck — of course, in your case, that works out to 49 years."

"Chief say,
'Someone...here...walk...through...buffalo...field.'"

"Well, that does it for my tomatoes."

"Well, this is getting nowhere fast."

Impolite as they were, the other bears could never help staring at Larry's enormous deer gut.

"Yes, yes...now don't fuss...I have something for you all."

What really happened to Elvis

When chickens dream

"Well, guess who's home a little early from today's castle siege?"

Continental drift whiplash

Kangaroo nerds

Classroom afflictions

Early Man

Sled Chickens of the North

"Well, down I go."

Songwriters of the Old West

How social animals work together

"It's the same dream night after night...I walk out on my web, and suddenly a foot sticks — and then another foot sticks, and another, and another, and another..."

"Yeah. My boss don't appreciate me either. To him I'm just a gofer. 'Igor! Go for dead bodies!...Igor! Go for brains!...Igor! Go for dead bodies!' I dunno — give me another beer."

Left to right: Old Man Winter, River, and Higgins

Headhunter hall closets

Onward they pushed, through the thick, steamy jungle, separately ruing the witch doctor's parting words: "Before you leave this valley, each of you will be wearing a duck."

"Listen — just take one of our brochures and see what we're all about....In the meantime, you may wish to ask yourself, 'Am I a happy cow?'"

"So tell us, Buffy…. How long have you been a talking dog?"

Flora practical jokes

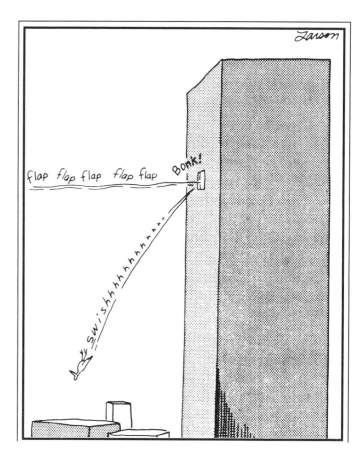

Nerds in hell

Canine comedians

"Somethin's up, Jake.... That's Ben Potter's horse, all right, but ain't that Henry Morgan's chicken ridin' him?"

"And so I ask the jury...is that the face of a mass murderer?"

Breakfast on other planets

No man is an island.

"What the hey?...Someone's shortsheeted my bed again!"

"You idiot! Don't write that down — his name ain't Puddin' Tame!"

"Bird calls! Bird calls, you fool!...Not mountain lions."

"Oh, boy! The 'Nerd'!...Now my collection's complete!"

Another unsubstantiated photograph of the Loch Ness monster (taken by Reuben Hicks, 5/24/84, Chicago)

"I don't know what you're insinuating, Jane, but I haven't seen your Harold all day — besides, surely you know I would only devour my *own* husband!"

Knowing the lions' preference for red meat, the spamalopes remained calm but wary.

Evening on a beached whale

"Dang, that gives me the creeps....I wish she'd hurry up and scoop that guy out."

"Well, the defendant and I had made this deal in which we both prospered...One of those 'you-scratch-me-behind-my-ears-I'll-scratch-you-behind-yours' arrangements."

Animal Camouflage

Piglet practical jokes

Cartoon teen-agers

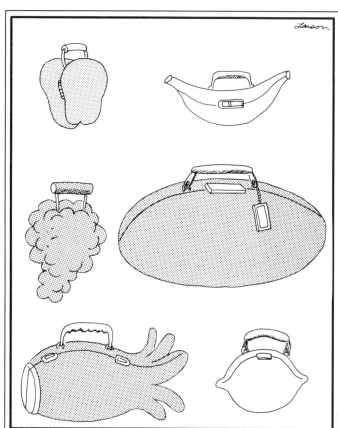

Fruitcases

"I'm *talking* to you!... You're so...so...so thick-membraned
sometimes."

When ornithologists are mutually attracted

"Primordial soup again?"

Rock Shop 101

"Hey, you wanna see a *real* scar?
Check *this* baby out!"

How bears relax

Dog threat letters

"You idiot! We want the scent on the pillow!
On the pillow!"

"Nuclear warheads, huh?...More like *defused* nuclear
warheads, if you ask me!"

The squid family on vacation

Amoeba porn flicks

"Here are the blueprints. Now look: This is going to be the *Liberty* Bell, so we obviously expect that it be forged with great diligence and skill."

"Oh, don't be silly! No thanks needed. Just take the brain — but tell that doctor you work for not to be such a stranger."

"Uh-oh, Stan...I guess it wasn't a big, blue mule deer."

At the popular dog film, *Man Throwing Sticks*

"Donald...Trade you a thorax and six legs for two of your segments."

"Think about it, Ed....The class Insecta contains 26 orders, almost 1,000 families, and over 750,000 described species—but I can't shake the feeling we're all just a bunch of bugs."

Dog Hell

Metamorphosis Nightclubs

Parakeet furniture

Humpty Dumpty's final days

Medusa starts her day.

Hell's library

Just as Dale entered the clearing and discovered, standing together, the Loch Ness monster, Bigfoot, and Jackie Onassis, his camera jammed.

"Coincidence, ladies and gentlemen? Coincidence that my client just *happened* to live across from the A-1 Mask Co., just *happened* to walk by their office windows each day, and they, in turn, just *happened* to stumble across this new design?"

At the Old Spiders' Home

Braving the Indian "pillow" gauntlet

Unbeknownst to most historians, Einstein started down the road of professional basketball before an ankle injury diverted him into science.

"A few cattle are going to stray off in the morning, and tomorrow night a stampede is planned around midnight. Look, I gotta get back....Remember, when we reach Santa Fe, I ain't slaughtered."

Poodles of the Serengeti

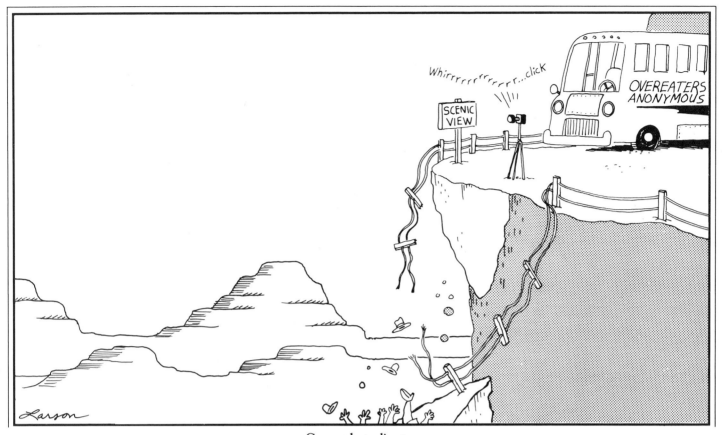

Group photo disasters

"Indians!"

Appliance healers

Elephant campfires

"Remember the...uh...Remember the...Remember that place in Texas!"

"OK. I'll go back and tell my people that you're staying in the boat, but I warn you they're *not* going to like it."

Full moon and empty head

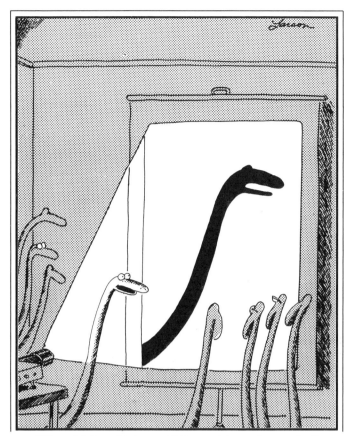

"Now this is…this is…well, I guess it's another snake."

"It's a letter from Julio in America….His banana bunch arrived safely and he's living in the back room of some grocery store."

"Oh, wait! Wait, Cory!…Add the cereal *first* and *then* the milk!"

Deer grandmothers

Early microbiologists

With their parents away, the young dragons would stay up late lighting their sneezes.

An impressionable moment in the childhood of Buffalo Bill

Same planet, different worlds

"Green blood? I *hate* green blood."

"This is getting pretty eerie, Simmons.... Another skull, another fortune."

"Oh, for heaven's sake! Your father left in such a hurry this morning he's lost another antenna."

The portrait of Dorian Cow

"Maybe we should write that spot down."

The birth of jazz

The last thing a fly ever sees

The Greystokes at marriage counseling

Testing whether fish have feelings

Bird cellars

"Larry? Betty?...Stand up, will ya?...These are some friends
of mine, folks, who flew all the way in from the dump."

"Mind? Hey, buddy, these flat feet kept me out of the Army!"

Jazz at the Wool Club

Cartoon readings

"Mom! The kids at school say we're a family of
Nerdenthals!...Is that true?"

"Clean it up? Clean it up? Criminy, it's *supposed* to be
a rathole!"

The Potatoheads in Paris

Dial-a-Cat

Beginning duck

The Lone Ranger, long since retired, makes an unpleasant discovery.

All day long, a tough gang of astrophysicists would monopolize the telescope and intimidate the other researchers.

"When I got home, Harold's coat and hat were gone, his worries were on the doorstep, and Gladys Mitchell, my neighbor, says she saw him heading west on the sunny side of the street."

"Ooo! Now here's a nice one we built last fall."

Where beef jerky comes from

"Oh! *Four* steps to the left and *then* three to the right!...
What kind of dance was *I* doing?"

The ghost of Baron Rudolph von Guggenheim, 16th-century
nobleman murdered by the Countess Rowena DuBois
and her lover (believed to be the Duke of Norwood),
falls into Edna's bean dip.

Where we get fat

"Do I like it? Do I *like* it? ... Dang it, Thelma, you know my feelings on barbed wire."

When a body meets a body comin' through the rye

Primitive fandango

"Now go to sleep, Kevin — or once again I'll have to knock three times and summon the Floating Head of Death."

"Doesn't have buck teeth, doesn't have buck teeth, doesn't have…"

Tarzan is greeted by the Parakeet People.

School for the Mechanically Declined

"You know, I wish you'd get rid of that hideous thing — and I think it's just plain dangerous to have one in the house."

"Nik! The fireflies across the street — I think they're mooning us!"

"Louis…phonecaw."

Tantor burns up on I-90.

16th-century Mona wanna-bes

Suddenly, throwing the festivities into utter confusion, Ujang begins to play "Stardust."

"Hold it right there, Henry!... You ain't plannin' on takin' that wrinkled horse into town, are you?"

"Bummer of a birthmark, Hal."

Where all the young farm animals go to smoke

"Now, here's a feature you folks would really enjoy...
Voilà! A tree right off the master bedroom."

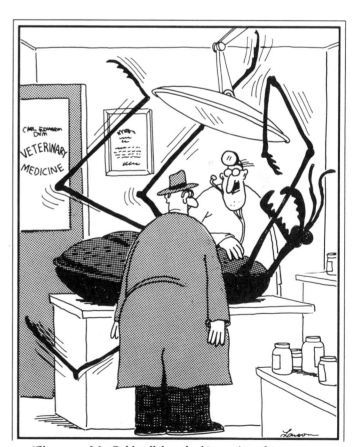

"I'm sorry, Mr. Caldwell, but the big guy's on his way out.
If you want my opinion, take him home, find a quiet spot
out in the yard, and squash him."

"No, wait! *That's* not Uncle Floyd! Who is that?...Criminy, I think it's just an air bubble!"

"Well, that about does it for the nose — I'm starting to hit cartilage."

"Frankly, you've got a lot of anger toward the world to work out, Mr. Pembrose."

"So, Raymond...Linda tells us you work in the security division of an automobile wreckage site."

"Listen. We may be young, but we're in love, and we're getting married — I'll just work until Jerry pupates."

The committee to decide whether spawning should be taught in school

"OK, OK, you guys have had your chance — the horses want another shot at it."

"Ah, yes, Mr. Frischberg, I thought you'd come... but which of us is the *real* duck, Mr. Frischberg, and not just an illusion?"

When crows dream

Buffalo dares

"You're sick, Jessy!…Sick, sick, sick!"

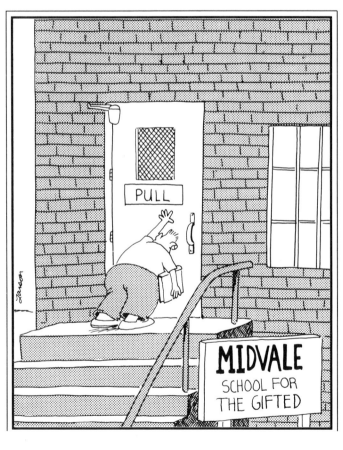

"You sure you're supposed to be doin' that, Mitch?"

African rakesnake

"Horse!…Is there a man called 'Horse' in here?"

"Hold it right there, Frank!…If you're gonna shake, you do it in another room!"

"Now!…*That* should clear up a few things around here!"

Baryshnikov's ultimate nightmare

"Wheeeeeeeeeeeeee!"

"I wonder if you could help me…I'm looking for
523 West Cherry and…Oh! Wow! Deja vu!"

And for two excruciating months, he was simply known as
"Skinhead of the Jungle."

Seconds later, Mrs. Norton was covered with ink.

When potato salad goes bad

The door swung wide, and there, to the horror of the other pirates, stood Captain Monet — unmistakable with his one eye and pegbody.

"Just a word of warning, Myron — if you miss, I'm comin' after your big hazel."

Night of the Living Dead Chipmunks

"Hey! C'mon, Jed!...Ease up on them hammers!"

"MY reflection? Look at YOURS, Randy...You look like some big fat swamp thing."

"Hey, I'm not *crazy*...sure, I let him drive once in a while, but he's never, *never* off this leash for even a second."

Thomas Sullivan, a blacksmith who attended the original Thanksgiving dinner, is generally credited as being the first person to stick olives on all his fingers.

The Grim Reaper as a child

The old "fake harpoon" gag

"Oh, lovely — just the hundredth time you've managed to cut everyone's head off."

"Be firm, Arnold…Let them in once and they'll expect it every time."

"Anytime, Slim."

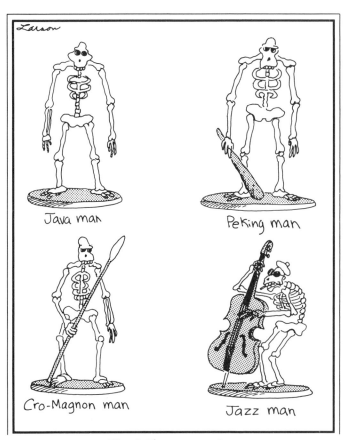

Hominid reconstructions

Suddenly, everyone turned and looked — there, standing in the doorway, was one wretched, mean-looking ingrown.

"OK, let's see… That's a curse on you, a curse on you, and a curse on you."

Snake inventors

Insectosaurs

"Well, from across the hall I could hear this heated argument, followed by sounds of a scuffle. Suddenly there was this tremendous, blood-curdling 'quaaaaaacck!' That's when I called."

Witch doctor waiting rooms

Gong birds

Single-cell bars

"Hey! They're edible!...This changes everything!"

Back-hump drivers

"Well, that does it! Look at our furniture! The Shuelers have visited us for the last time!"

"Allen, you jerk! Dad told us not to do that or we'd scare the fish!"

Only they know the difference.

"Airrrrr spearrrr…airrrrr spearrrr!…"

"Excuse me, sir, but Shinkowsky keeps stepping on my sandal."

"Dang, if it doesn't happen every time!…We just sit down to relax and someone's knockin' at the door."

Wendall Zurkowitz: Slave to the waffle light

Early clock-watchers

"Hey! That's milk! And you said you were all empty, you stinkin' liar!"

"He's dead, all right — beaked in the back...and, you know, this won't be easy to solve."

"Quick, Abdul! Desert!...One 's' or two?"

"That's a lie, Morty!...Mom says you might have got the brains in the family, but *I* got the looks!"

That evening, with her blinds pulled, Mary had three helpings of corn, two baked potatoes, extra bread, and a little lamb.

"Just think...Here we are, the afternoon sun beating down on us, a dead, bloated rhino underfoot, and good friends flying in from all over...I tell you, Ed, this is the best of times."

"No, they're not real exciting pets — mostly they just lie around and wait to be fed — although a couple years ago Charles tried teachin' him to take a cookie from his mouth."

"He's got one shot left, Murray — and then he's *ours!*"

Unknown to most historians, William Tell had an older and less fortunate son named Warren.

God as a kid tries to make a chicken in his room.

As the first duck kept Margaret's attention, the second one made its move.

"Yes! Yes! That's it!…Just a little higher."

"Uh-oh!…Stuart blew his air sac!"

"Skunk sandwich, Bill…mmmmm…skunk sandwich.
…Trade for that banana?"

"I'm sorry, ma'am, but his license does check out and, after
all, your husband *was* in season. Remember, just because he
knocks doesn't mean you have to let him in."

"Here comes another big one, Roy, and here — we — goooooowheeeeeeeooo!"

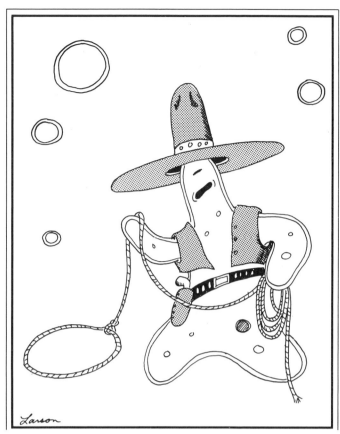

"So, until next week — Adios, amoebas."

"I tell you, a crib is just plain worthless — what we need around here is a good cardboard box."

"Oh my gosh, Linda!…I think your Barbie's contemplating suicide!"

Punk flamingoes

"Second floor, please."

"And another thing! I'm sick and tired of you callin' me 'new kid' all the time!"

"Look. Why don't you just give yourself up quietly?...Otherwise, this thing could turn into a frenzy — and nobody wants that."

Bobo remained free the rest of his life, although he did find it necessary to seek counseling.

"Maybe it's *not* me, y'know?...Maybe it's the *rest* of the herd that's gone insane."

"We're gettin' old, Jake."

Through a gross navigational error, the Love Boat steams into the Strait of Hormuz.

Circa 300 B.C.: The first barbarian invader reaches the Great Wall of China

"Whoa! *That* was a good one! Try it, Hobbs — just poke his brain right where my finger is."

The famous "Mr. Ed vs. Francis the Talking Mule" debates

"Go back to sleep, Chuck. You're just havin' a nightmare — of course, we *are* still in hell."

"Look. I'm sorry…If you weighed 500 pounds, we'd certainly accommodate you — but it's simply a fact that a 400-pound gorilla does *not* sleep anywhere he wants to."

"Criminy!…It seems like every summer there's more and more of these things around!"

"See Dick run. See Jane run. Run run run. See the wolves chase Dick and Jane. Chase chase chase…"

"For God's sake, hurry, driver!…She's dropping babies all over the place!"

The conversation had been brisk and pleasant when, suddenly and simultaneously, everyone just got dog tired.

"I don't mean to exacerbate this situation, Roger, but I think I'm quite close to bursting into maniacal laughter and imagining that your nose is really a German sausage."

Wildlife preserves

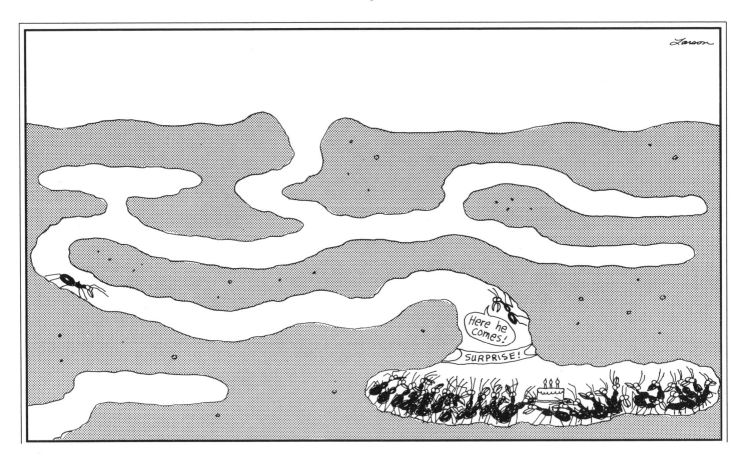

"Give me a hand, here, Etta...I got into a nest of wiener dogs over on Fifth and Maple."